SOLITUDE & SUNSHINE

To Bill Bass,
whose book this really is

SOLITUDE & SUNSHINE

IMAGES · OF · A · GRAND · CANYON · CHILDHOOD

By Stephen G. Maurer based on conversations with William G. Bass

PRUETT P PUBLISHING COMPANY
Boulder, Colorado

EB

First Edition
1 2 3 4 5 6 7 8 9

Printed in the United States of America

Library of Congress Cataloging in Publication Data

Maurer, Stephen G.
   Solitude and Sunshine: Images of a Grand Canyon Childhood.

   1. Bass, William G., 1900-   . 2. Grand
Canyon Register (Ariz.) — Social life and customs.
3. Tourist trade — Arizona — Grand Canyon Region —
History — 20th century. 4. Grand Canyon Region
(Ariz.) — Biography. I. Title
F788.B29 1983   979.1'32C.52   82-20486
ISBN 0-87108-639-5

Introduction

This is a book of memories. At the end of a long life Bill Bass looked back on his childhood and remembered. Time, eighty years worth of time, had draped the past in a haze; people and events move in those fog-days of the long ago on a measured, even plane. There are no sharp edges, no great joys and no great sorrows, for it is the prerogative of the very old to gloss over squabbles and say: "This is what I remember, this is what I *want* to remember."

Central in these stories is the figure of Bill's father William Wallace Bass, one of the first and most important settlers on the south rim of the Grand Canyon. In fact, this book is as much about him as about Bill. A man of indefatigable energy, W. W. Bass came to the town of Williams, Arizona, in 1883. He had been working on the elevated railway in New York City but moved west on account of his ill health. In 1884 he located a camp on the south rim, some twenty-seven miles west of present-day Grand Canyon Village. The following year he began advertising for the tourist trade.

Bass first built a stage road to his camp from Williams. Then, in 1891, another road from Ashfork. In 1895 he married Ada Diefendorf, a schoolteacher from East Worcester, New York. She bore him four children: three daughters and a son.

By the time the railroad arrived at the Canyon in 1901, Bass Camp and its proprietor were well known. A steady flow of tourists had visited there, among them the painter Thomas Moran, John Muir, Zane Grey, and George Peabody. George Wharton James, the prolific author of travel books and Frederic H. Maude, a noted landscape photographer became good friends of the family and returned year after year.

The main house at Bass Camp stood less than a hundred feet from the Canyon's brink, and it was in this milieu, superimposed on one of the world's most awe-inspiring sceneries, that the Bass children grew up. Indians, tourists, horses, burros, wagons and stages, the solitude and isolation of Bass Camp fill Bill Bass' earliest memories. He was the second child, born in 1900, four years after his sister Edith. He was but one and one-half years old when taken into the Canyon for the first time, across the Colorado River in a canvas boat to Shinumo Creek where he and his parents spent the next two months trying to escape the cold on the rim above. They lived in a canvas tent near the garden that Bill's father planted. Bass prospected along Shinumo Creek, and Bill took his first, tentative steps that forever would bring him back to the Canyon.

The Bass children learned fast. Edith was three and one-half years old when she rode horseback all the way from the rim to the river; Bill repeated the feat at the same age on the back of a burro. The two rode down, alone and unescorted, when Edith was nine and Bill but five, to bring up horses left at the river. By then all the places along the seven-mile-long trail were familiar and known to them. Mystic Spring, on the sandstone plateau, 1,500 feet below the rim, a favorite stay for the tourist parties their father had conducted into the Canyon in the early days but by now hardly used anymore; Rock Camp, a U-shaped overhang twenty minutes from the Colorado, full of tools and equipment; the small cove by the river where the canvas and wooden boats were kept. Three miles to the west the mine in Copper Canyon where Bass' men sank shafts of hope into backbreaking granite; across the river the asbestos mine in Hakatai Canyon;

the camp on Shinumo Creek with its garden and fruit trees, Belgian hares and chickens, and brush-moustached, tobacco-juice-spitting John Waltenberg tending them all. Beyond the Shinumo lay the mysterious world of the north rim, which they knew only from stories: the lush meadows, tall forests, and abundant deer. They knew all these and much more, the curiosities along the trail, cliff dwellings and rock formations, rattlesnakes and scorpions. It was their world.

Life in that world was not easy. Water and feed for the animals were equally scarce—stock was left to wander in search of both, and endless hours were spent rounding them up again. Edith and Bill learned to ride and throw a lariat as a matter of course. Williams, the nearest town, was seventy miles away, and going to the post office at Grand Canyon Village meant a round trip of fifty miles. If the roads were dry. Because when it rained, it rained with a vengeance and the roads became bottomless seas of mud that wore down man and beast alike.

The railroad came to the Canyon when Bill was one year old. The days of the long stage rides were over. Bass had established a siding, five miles from the railroad's terminus, where tourists bound for Bass Camp could disembark. In 1906 he built there what the family came to call the "White House." By then the other two children, Hazel and Mabel, had also been born. For the next five years the family moved back and forth from Bass Camp to the White House during the tourist season. In the same year he built the White House, Bass strung two cables across the Colorado River at the foot of his trail, in order to gain access to the north side during the spring runoff. In 1908 he added two more cables and a cage capable of carrying livestock across.

Under the primitive conditions of the south rim, formal education was, at best, a haphazard affair. Come fall, Ada Bass and the children would move to Williams or Phoenix—even to Los Angeles, and enroll Edith and Bill in school. These educational forays were usually short-lived: in a couple of months the family would be back at the Canyon. Then, come January, the process would be repeated. By 1911 there were enough children at the Grand Canyon to start a school—the Bass family supplied half of the required minimum attendance. Bass had built a new house less than a mile from the railroad terminal. The exterior walls were covered with pressed tin, and soon the family referred to it as the "Tin House."

The silence and isolation of Bass Camp was now replaced with the hubbub of the small community. Trains arrived and departed daily with an ever increasing number of tourists, the Bass children went to school, the first automobiles appeared. Bass himself had bought one in 1914. He had foreseen the profound changes trains and cars would bring to the tourist business, how the leisurely tours of the past would be replaced by short sightseeing trips centered around the railroad's terminus. Rim drives became a favorite way of seeing the Canyon, and soon Bass had six surreys and an automobile taking tourists on drives. It was worth it: in the exceptionally good year of 1915 he grossed over $20,000.

And the tourists kept coming. An intense competition for the visitors' trade developed between the Santa Fe Railway's Fred Harvey Company and independent operators like Bass, a competition complete with private detectives, fistfights, threats, and lawsuits. One by one the others were driven out of business, but Bass held on. He was at his height, a respected though not universally liked figure at the Canyon. He had just sold his asbestos mine and was about to build another cable crossing for the new owners. He was well known and aware, as he once wrote, that "my name can never be erased from the Canyon's history."

It was all about to end. Edith, who wrangled horses and took tourists on rim drives and trail rides, married in 1917. In that same year Bill went to work for the Fred Harvey Company as a driver. He had done his share in the family business, had worked down in the copper mine and had helped with the packtrains that brought the ore out. He had worked on the trails in the Canyon ever since he could remember, mattock and shovel were his constant companions.

But he was also the child of a new era. He knew horses and burros, he had grown up with them, but it was the automobile that fascinated him. He had received his chauffeur's license when he was only sixteen, and now opportunity beckoned. It was time to break away from home. The long line of Fred Harvey's Pierce Arrows stood ready each morning, their uniformed drivers in long leather dusters waiting. There would be pretty girls among the tourists and people from all walks of life—you did not need to travel, for the world came to you. And in the evening, after the last party returned dazed with the beauty of sunset from Hopi Point, the drivers would stroll along the rim, hoping to renew acquaintances made earlier in the day. There would be a dance somewhere, the gaming tables at Rowe's Well, there would be moonlight and always the sheer, overwhelming beauty of the Canyon. It was a good life, to be a Fred Harvey driver at seventeen.

William Wallace Bass was sixty-nine years old in 1917. He had watched the Canyon become the major tourist attraction he predicted it would. Indeed, he played an important part in its development. He had seen it change from open land to forest reserve, to national monument, each change bringing more regulations, more restrictions. He was about to see one more: in 1917 the National Park Service was established and two years later Grand Canyon became a national park. He also realized that he could not compete with the Fred Harvey Company which, in 1920, became the principal concessionaire at the Canyon. Like many westerners, Bass too, abhorred monopolies, whether the government's, the railroad's, or Fred Harvey's; but there was nothing he could do. In 1923, at the age of seventy-five, he closed his business and three years later sold his holdings to the Santa Fe Land and Development Company.

The two trees still stand where the trail drops off the rim. A faint path snakes out to Surprise Point, past where the tent cabins once stood, past the round corral now overgrown with sage. The buildings are all gone, only the rock foundations are visible still: John's cabin . . . the woodshed . . . the barn. There was laughter here once, laughter and cries. Stages pulled in coming over the last rise by the hill, often after dark, sometimes in driving snowstorms. Cold, frozen hands fumbled for a door, for a match, until wood crackled in the stoves and the windows began to glow. Outside lanterns flickered in the darkness, and feeding horses blew clouds of steam into the air.

It is so quiet. An errant breeze rustles rusted tin cans near the cistern. Bill's voice comes floating on the air, that dreamy voice of looking back with a story-telling lilt in it: "I remember, I remember one time. . . ."

Bass Camp, 1981

Looking north from the Esplanade below Bass Camp. Hakatai Canyon, where William Wallace Bass' asbestos mine was located, is center left; Copper Canyon is barely discernible on the lower right. Photograph by Frederic H. Maude, circa 1896.

I don't remember when I first saw the Canyon—you see, for me it has always been there. I envy people their first look at it. I never had that.

Tourists along the south rim. Date and photographer unknown.

9

Those two pinon trees on the rim — if they could talk, they could tell many stories. So could the bench where guests sat to watch the evening light and the shadows. After sundown warm breezes came out of the Canyon. It was a nice place to sit.

Nearly every evening, after supper, my Dad would gather there with the guests, reciting poetry or telling stories of his life. How often have I listened to them! I could almost repeat them word for word as though they happened to me. They became a part of my life.

John Waltenberg and Jane C. Seymour by the twin trees at Bass Camp. Photograph by Levi or Dorothy Noble, 1916.

I often think back to the days when we lived on the rim of the Canyon—Dad, my Mother, my sisters Edith, Hazel, Mabel, and I. It was a rather beautiful life because we could run and play and do as we liked out there on the rim with no one to bother us; no noises, streetcars, airplanes, or anything. And so we had a rather lonesome life, but it wasn't really lonesome because we had so much to think about all the time—we gathered wildflowers, we found arrowheads, we built imaginary farms and ranches with barns and corrals. Wild buckwheat stems would be our mares, another plant the stallions, small sticks of different colors our colts. Yucca stems that had moisture in them would be our cows.

We lived at the Canyon, we loved the Canyon, we appreciated it all, we didn't look at it like just a big hole in the ground. . . .

The Bass children at Bass Camp, circa 1908. From left to right: Edith, Hazel, Bill, and Mabel. Photograph by W. W. Bass.

I think my Mother liked living at the Canyon, but then again, maybe she didn't, because of the primitive conditions there. It was a rugged life. But she always came back for more. . . . My sister Edith was born at her Mother's place in East Worcester, New York, but she returned after three years, and twelve months later I was born. And later, of course, four years later, came my sister Hazel, and in eighteen months Mabel who was also born back east. If she hadn't enjoyed living at the Canyon, I don't know why she kept coming back for more.

I took her to the north rim when she was in her eighties. She sat on the porch at the lodge for a long time, watching the Canyon, looking at things only her eyes saw. And then she spoke, as if answering a question that echoed across the years: "I love the Canyon, too."

Ada Diefendorf Bass with Darky on the south rim around 1920. Photographer unknown.

I thought about that the other day, how my Mother and we kids were left alone there on the rim, for weeks on and more. Not knowing when Dad would come in, sometimes running low on food and water. How night after night we would lie in bed and listen for the sound of stage wheels, wondering when he would come home.

Or waiting by the window, in the bright sunshine of the day, waiting, always waiting. . . .

Ada Bass and Bill at Bass Camp with Havasupai Indians. Photograph by W. W. Bass, 1902.

And the excitement when we would hear him in the night, hear the hard stage tires strike rock up by the hill. We'd get up and light the light and fix beds for everybody, and sometimes we kids would have to move out of our beds to make room for the tourists, sleep on the floor if he brought too many people, sleep on the floor or out in the tents. . . .

Bass stage leaving Bass Camp, W. W. Bass driving. Date and photographer unknown.

Bass Ca

It would have been nice if we could have gone away to school, but then, we might have learned the wrong things. My Father taught us about nature, the things that the Canyon taught us too, instead of books. Like geology and fossils. I used to study fossils when I was a boy. Of course, that led me to wonder how one of those things had lived many years ago, and how they were so well preserved in the rocks. How they tell the story of life as it was on earth at that time. So I got to thinking as I looked around our house on the Canyon's rim, I got to thinking that some day in the future somebody will be digging in the limestone and find one of the things we had, all embedded in the rock, and wonder what we were like.

Tourists at Bass Camp. Author George Wharton James is on the extreme left, W. W. Bass is third from the right. Date and photographer unknown.

On the trail in Bass Canyon. Photograph by F. H. Maude, circa 1900.

Rock Camp. Photograph by F. H. Maude or George Wharton James, circa 1899.

Camp on the Esplanade below Bass Camp. Photograph by F. H. Maude, 1898.

We all loved to go with my Dad when he went on hikes with the tourists. The trail leads from Bass Camp and follows the rim through the forest to Havasupai Point, the most beautiful place on the south rim where the Canyon is sixteen miles wide and drops off almost straight down to the river. Where on most quiet days you can hear the rapids below. And as we walked along the rim, my Dad would pick leaves and twigs and things to pass back to the line of people following him, and tell what they were and always had a story about them. He would stop and gather a circle around a certain plant or tree or something, and tell about it.

He would tell about the pack rats that build their nests of sticks. He called them trade rats, because they come and take something from your house and always leave something in place of it. He would tell that one time at Bass Camp my Mother left some silverware out and when she got back she had a pile of sticks instead—a rat had taken all the spoons and forks and put them in its nest.

And so we learned, and his stories got us interested in the world around us.

Looking north from the Esplanade below Bass Camp. Grand Scenic Divide on the right. Photograph by F. H. Maude, 1896.

As time went on, each of us became entirely different in our concepts of life. We each enjoyed different things. Take Edith, for instance, my oldest sister. Her life was strictly horses. She was always planning the day when she'd have a ranch and a herd of horses of her own. My Dad gave her several horses. The first one was Daisy, a mare with a spindly-legged colt who could run like the wind. She named him Ranger.

Edith became a very good horsewoman. She could ride horses the rest of us couldn't. The men who worked for us would always praise her above me, just to tease me. They would say: "Why, Edith can ride a horse where you can't drag a rope." Of course, they were just trying to get on the good side of her.

Edith and Bill Bass at Bass Camp with Daisy *and her colt* Ranger. *Photograph by W. W. Bass, 1907.*

We had a rather spirited horse called Fox, who'd sometimes take the notion to run away, take the bit between his teeth and hold it so you couldn't get him to do anything. He'd just run like the dickens. One time he ran away with Edith, ran underneath some trees and bent her back, threw her right over the saddle. She lay on the ground for quite a while. Finally, she came to and managed to catch the horse again and walked him in to Bass Camp. Her back was in bad shape for a long time, it hurt her something terrible for about a year or so. We didn't go to the doctor about it—they didn't have any doctors there.

One day she was riding another horse down at the White House and at the fence gate, why, somebody had put a wire across. She didn't know it was there, and she was riding, coming up very fast. Well, the horse didn't see it till it got right to it and stopped suddenly, throwing her over the saddle. Luckily it did not bruise her much or hurt her much. She cut her face though, and she always had a scar there. But after that she had no more trouble with her back—her back was healed.

I often went out and sat on the rim and just looked and listened. Watched the birds, the changing colors, and the shadows. And listened, listened to the Canyon. To the various sounds. Like the swifts swooping past the rim, and other birds too as they flew by, to the burros braying far down below. And every now and then I'd hear the faint roar of a rockslide somewhere.

One evening during the summertime, it was about dusk and I was sitting out there when a bright light appeared, like a falling star, right over the river to the west, halfway across the Canyon. It lit up the whole sky, and after it hit there was a loud noise like an explosion, and for a long time I heard rock rolling. . . .

View of the Esplanade below Bass Camp. Bass Canyon is in the center of the picture. Photograph by F. H. Maude, 1896.

I had a hobby of rolling rocks into the Canyon. That's before we realized there was any harm in it. I rolled down rocks that weighed tons it seems, straining myself prying them loose. And they'd go right down, cutting a path through the trees! We'd try to get them to roll from the top down to and over the Coconino wall.

We would go out on Havasupai Point, where the rocks would fall for thousands of feet you know, a straight drop of three thousand feet! It was fun! No law against it then. Every now and then I have dreams that I'm out rolling rocks, and one of those rangers is going to catch me.

When I was out on Havasupai Point a few years ago, I took the chance of rolling a couple of rocks down, just to show the friends that were with me how we used to do it. And the echo of those rocks going down was very thrilling. That was one of the best times.

Havasupai Point. Photograph by F. H. Maude, 1898.

35

My Dad was down in Havasu Canyon one time when one of the Indians, old Tom, died. And the Supais had to burn him, as was their custom, and burn everything with him. All his possessions. Well, Tom had given my Dad this horse Silver, many years ago, and now he was really afraid that Tom's relatives wanted to get that horse back, steal it back, and burn it with Tom so he'd have something to ride in the afterworld.

So my Father had to take Silver down into the Canyon and swim him across to the other side and leave him there on the Shinumo, so the Indians couldn't get him. He was a pretty old horse by then, and he died along the trail over there, along the trail on Shinumo Creek.

Shinumo Creek. Photograph by F. H. Maude, circa 1898.

37

Edith was psychic. She had a premonition of things, she'd dream of them. One time I lost my favorite knife and couldn't find it. Edith got up one morning, went outside, walked right over to it and picked it up off the ground. She dreamt where it was.

My Dad was that way, too. One time he was building a water tank down on Cataract. As he was running the slip scraper, he stopped and said to the fellow working with him: "Take over for me, I have to go to Williams, my mother just died." And so he got on his horse and rode thirty-five miles to Williams where a telegram was waiting, telling him his mother had died.

"The Old Lunch Tree" between Bass Camp and the Caves. Date and photographer unknown.

One day when Edith woke up in the morning, she said: "We better keep watch today, I had a dream last night that a man came." And sure enough, around ten o'clock we saw this man come down the road, walking in sort of a zigzagging manner. He wasn't walking straight. We could tell he wasn't in his right mind by the way he walked, and we were all scared. My Mother got all of us, put us in the house, and shut the door. We were all alone there.

There was a rain barrel at the corner of the house that caught the water running off the roof when it rained. This man came up to it and tried to drink out of the barrel but couldn't reach the water. So then he came over and knocked on the door. My Mother opened it and asked him what he wanted. And he said, "I want a drink of water. I just had some water along the road but I am thirsty again."

Apparently he drank at the cisterns a mile away, because later we found that the lock was broken. Being so long without water on a hot day, then drinking cold water, helped perhaps to make him go out of his mind.

And so, after he'd drunk the water, my Mother asked him where he was going. He said, "I'm trying to go over where the Indians live." She said, "All right, I'll fix you a little lunch, because it is a long way down there." And so she fixed him some sandwiches and put it all in a white bag. But instead of going back the road the way he should have gone, he started out in the wrong direction. And my Mother said to him, "That isn't the way to go, you want to go back the way you came and follow down that way." He said, "That's all right, I'll be back in a little while." So that scared her.

Well, Harry Jennings was expected up from the Canyon sometime, and she was hoping he would come soon. She went out to the rim and hollered, and she could hear him answer, so she knew he would be up in a little bit. It was dark by then and there was a

The road to Bass Camp. Photograph by James Putnam, 1901.

41

bright moon shining. We were standing out on the rim watching Harry Jennings come up when she saw the white sack swinging in the moonlight as this fellow carried it in his hand. She ran into the house and got a lantern for Harry to take out to the corral to unload the burros.

The man saw the light in the corral and went there saying, "Hey, I found my way back, didn't I?" And Harry said, "Where the hell were you trying to go anyway?" The man replied, "I thought it was the ladies out here." So Harry says, "There is no ladies around here," and detained him talking while he got the burros and saddles unpacked, then they went over to the house. My Mother got them something to eat and fixed a bed for him out in the tin shack where we kept the saddles. Then he talked pretty irrational for a while. He was definitely deranged so, when he went to sleep in the tin shack, Harry locked him in there.

Next morning Harry Jennings was going to take him in and turn him over to the authorities. So he got a saddle horse for this man to ride and took him over to the forest ranger twenty miles away. They apparently let the man go, which they shouldn't have done, because it was thought he had set a fire, a forest fire, along the railroad tracks a few miles below there; and several days later they found him lying dead in a waterhole, his hands clutched to the waterhole where he was trying to get some water. . . .

Bass Camp in 1905. Photographer unknown.

Havasu Canyon. Photograph by F. H. Maude, circa 1898.

Havasupai Point. Photograph by James Putnam, 1901.

I remember my Dad had a book called *The Kite Trust*. It was about a boy whose father taught him how to make kites. He had a store where he sold them. He took the little boy in with him, and they called it The Kite Trust. I read the book and I made kites out of sticks and paper, and I used to fly them over the Canyon.

And I made parachutes out of paper, and on top of the parachutes I'd put a pin, bent over to hook on a part of the string I doubled, and the wind would take it up, took it up with the kite. And then I would pull the string back, like this, and it would pop them off, and the parachutes would go flying out over the Canyon.

View of the Canyon near Bass Camp. Photograph by F. H. Maude, 1896.

The Supais were famous for their orchards—they had the best peaches and apricots. Sometimes my Mother would go down there, to Havasu Canyon, to can fruit, taking the jars and everything down on burros. One year she came back with 140 jars.

Once I stayed a couple of months down there with Simmons, the agent who had a boy my age. We played together. I learned how to make bows and arrows, and I got so I could shoot just like the Supai kids. We'd put watermelons on the posts and shoot arrows into them. We sharpened sticks to put in the arrow shafts for points. And then I conceived the idea of taking some horseshoe nails and put those in the shafts instead. And the Supai kids had a run on the commissary for horseshoe nails. So I wasn't very popular with the agent for a while.

Orchard in Havasu Canyon. Date and photographer unknown.

49

When I got ready to leave, why, I was to come out with Mr. Simmons, the agent. They put me on a burro to ride out on, but when we got a few miles up the trail, there was a terrible rain and we met a flood coming down. The burro I was riding got on a high place in a wash, where the water came down on either side of an island, and just stood there. Well, the water was rising around us, beginning to come up over that island and soon it was knee high and the burro just stood there. The agent had a horse that could swim well, and he came out and put me on the back of the saddle and got me back to shore. And then we had to wait for the flood to come down, and I finally rode out on the back of the saddle behind this dirty old Indian, old Vesna; rode up there and out to the top.

Flood in Havasu Canyon. Photograph by F. H. Maude, circa 1898.

After the flood, before the trails were passable again, why, there was an earthquake, shaking the houses and everything. I was in the outhouse at the time, and as it was a kind of a flimsy old thing, I sat in there thinking that it would fall right in the hole with me inside. Tilted over that much, I thought of my Dad and my Mother and ran out—I was so scared I didn't even pull my pants up.

And the rocks were rolling down all over, and the Indians ran out shooting arrows up in the air to appease their gods to save the two big rocks, the *Wegeleywah*, because they believed that if those rocks ever fell off, it would be the end of the Supais. The two rocks called *Wegeleywah*.

Havasu Canyon showing the rocks Wegeleywah. *Photograph by George Wharton James or W. W. Bass, 1890s.*

Chickapanagi was my Father's favorite friend among the Indians. My Dad often took him to hunt on the north rim. He would give Chickapanagi his rifle and three shells, and Chick would come back with three deer.

He had a son, Jessie, that I grew up with. We played together a lot. One time, when we lived at the White House, Jessie came in and my Mother gave him a doughnut saying, "Jessie, don't eat the hole now." And he said, "No, I'll be very careful, I'll eat all around it and throw the hole in the Canyon."

Jessie passed away a short time ago. Most of my old Indian friends have passed on. . . .

Chickapanagi at Bass Camp. Photograph by W. W. Bass, date unknown.

The Indians ate pack rats. If we were cutting a log that had a rat's nest in it, and the Supais were around, why, they would come over and catch it. They'd dig a hole in the ground and build a fire. When they had enough coals, they'd put some in the bottom of the hole, then some rocks, and the rat on top of that, then more rocks and more coals and, finally, dirt on top. Then when noontime came, they'd dig it up and have roast rat. They cooked it without cleaning it. I was invited to have roast rat once, but when they uncovered the hole and I got one smell of it, I just about fainted. So I excused myself and told them I wasn't hungry.

Havasupai Indians in Havasu Canyon. Photograph by F. H. Maude, 1898.

My Dad had a couple of men painting the wagons at Bass Camp one time, and when they finished, they wanted to go to Supai. Well, John Waltenberg had just come out of the Canyon, so my Dad told them they could take the burros and pack outfit to go down, ride down there. I went with them too. We camped that night down in Havasu Canyon and saw the village the next day. When we started back, why, one of the men saw a nest, what he thought might be an eagle's nest high up on the wall, and he wanted to go over and shoot at it. He asked me to go with him so he told the other fellow to just go on with the three pack burros. He did, and we went over there, and the man shot at the nest but missed.

We fooled around for a while then we went on up the trail, thinking the other fellow was ahead of us all the time, but he got off on another trail and when we got to the top, he wasn't there. And we waited and waited, but he didn't come and didn't come and didn't come. So we went on to Bass Camp because this fellow had the pack burros with all our grub, and all we had were the two burros we were riding.

A couple of days later here's this man come walking down the road—he had left the burros and the pack outfit someplace out on Great Thumb Mesa, lost them way out there someplace. He probably got too far to the left, to the west, and wandered out on the Great Thumb, up that way, and in that big country there, he couldn't find anything. He was lost, so he took the packs off and turned the burros loose, and we never did find the burros or the pack outfit again. Never did find it.

My Dad gave me a beautiful little horse, a pretty little black horse with a white blaze. A man who'd been working for us got ready to leave and he wanted to go down in the Canyon, down to the cable ferry. And he wanted to borrow my horse, so I loaned him my little horse to go down to the river. And that was the last I ever saw my horse.

He went on down, and he tied him up to a rock or a bush or something, near a cliff, while he went across the river and over to Shinumo. He'd left the rope too long and the horse got tangled up in it and fell over the cliff, killing himself.

I was sick about it.

The view upstream near the cable ferry. Bass rapid is on the left. Photograph by F. H. Maude, circa 1902.

We had been working on the cable crossing down in the Canyon, and after we got the cables secured, Harry Jennings, Morris Lauzon, and some of the others decided to go to the north rim to hunt. So they went, and John went with them too, but my Dad and I decided to go to the asbestos mine.

I remember we fished in the Colorado, and we had a couple of fishes we caught the day before, had them on one of the burros. We had three burros with us: two to ride and one to pack. But the trail was so bad, we walked most of the time. I was leading my riding burro, following behind the pack burro, and in one of the narrow places the pack hit the wall and threw the burro off balance so that his foot was over the ledge, over the edge of the wall. I had a hoe in my hand—we were working on the trail, working as we went along— and I took the hoe and put it under the burro's foot so he could get a hold and not fall over the cliff with all our packs on.

Then my Dad had a spell on the way to the mine and had to sit down a lot, resting on a rock with his hand over his heart. I was frightened. He had these spells that would come on for a while, then they'd be gone and he would be all right. Claimed it was caused by a plough handle hitting him in the chest when he was a child, and he felt that way ever since.

I had never been to the asbestos mine before, but that night we slept up in that canyon, above the mine shaft where a big boulder had fallen over and left a cave underneath, and we slept in that cave that night. And I remember we had the two fish for dinner.

On the Topacobya trail. Photograph by F. H. Maude, 1899.

63

We were always concerned about water. We had very little of it. Seems like it never rained though it rained all around us. So, we were always watching the clouds. I would see one of them on the horizon, moving across the Canyon, and I would try to get it to come our way. Sometimes we would go to bed at night seeing a little thunderhead come up. Why, we'd sit there all night praying to cause the wind to blow the cloud over to us.

The storms usually formed over the north rim. It seemed like they came north so easily. We could see the storms there and the water that came down from the clouds, and we hoped that they would move our way.

We watched more for clouds coming out of the south, from Cataract country. We'd hear about the floods down on Cataract— they had some really big storms down that way.

One night I saw a big old cloud there, south of us, and thought it would never get to us. I went to bed before it ever got there and watched the lightning, and sure enough, about twelve o'clock, it began to rain. . . .

Looking down Bass Canyon to the north rim. Photograph by F. H. Maude, date unknown.

We had a garden on the rim near Bass Camp. My Dad ploughed it all up one year, built a brush fence around it, and planted potatoes. For seed he'd just cut the eyes out of the potatoes and planted them where they'd grow. I thought that was real nice: potatoes planting little potatoes.

John suggested that we plant a row of potatoes and a row of onions: the onions would make the potatoes' eyes water and we wouldn't need any irrigation.

We had a garden down in the Canyon, too, across the river on Shinumo Creek. My Dad fixed up some prehistoric irrigation ditches there, and he had an orchard of fig trees, peaches, and apricots; and he grew corn, tomatoes, grapes, and melons—the best melons I've ever had.

During the runoff the river would come up sixty feet or more, sometimes sixteen feet in twenty-four hours. I had seen big logs come down and just break up in splinters in the rapids, and that's one reason why we had to build a cable crossing because in the summer, when the snows came down, the river would rise up that way and be full of driftwood floating, and we were afraid to go across in the boat. One summer the garden all died because we couldn't get across to water it.

Shinumo Camp. From left to right: W. W. Bass, John Waltenberg, Havasupai Indian. Date and photographer unknown.

We'd go down in the Canyon in the wintertime, during the heavy snows. Sometimes we went only as far as Rock Camp, on this side of the river, just to get out of the cold, but mostly we stayed on the Shinumo on the north side. My Dad and John would be off prospecting or working in the mines, and my Mother would stay with us.

One of our first camps on the Shinumo was below a big rock. My Mother was afraid that it would fall, so she had my Dad move the camp off a ways and sure enough, the next year that big rock fell right where the tent was.

Ada Bass and Bill on the divide above Shinumo Creek. Photograph by W. W. Bass, circa 1910.

Bass Camp was at a lower elevation than Bright Angel, and we didn't have the snows they had over there—we had snow but not as much. So we always used wagons, even in the wintertime, but when we shod the horses we'd put shoes with little spikes on them.

It took a lot of energy just to keep the stoves going, to keep them hot and to be warm. It was my job to see that there was plenty of wood. The kitchen stove took a different size stick than the heating stoves, and the one in the big dining room had a larger firebox which took even bigger pieces. My Dad made me a wheelbarrow for hauling wood when the ground was dry or frozen. I remember how he made the wheel for the wheelbarrow by taking the lids of two nail kegs and nailing them together, which left a groove in the center where he put a piece of rope for a tire. For the winter, when there was snow on the ground, he built me a small sled to haul the wood in.

We didn't have any place to go sledding at Bass Camp, but later, at the Tin House, there was a hill where we could coast down, coast down on one of those big scoop shovels, get on a scoop shovel and ride the handle. We'd sit down with the handle in front of our leg and pull up the front, keep pulling the handle and go riding, scooting around. . . .

Winter at Bass Camp. Photograph by W. W. Bass, 1904.

75

Every time we moved, back and forth from one place to another; from the White House to the Tin House to Bass Camp, my Mother's piano would have to go, too.

Most every evening we'd get together, especially if we had company, and my Mother would play the piano and Dad the violin. And we'd sing. One of our favorite tunes was an old song, "Waiting For The Wagon." That was one we sang a lot. And "Old Black Joe" and "Silver Bell"—all kinds of old songs.

The Tin House. W. W. Bass in the surrey, Ada Bass on the porch. Circa 1915.
Photographer unknown.

The White House. Date and photographer unknown.

Pack burros at the Tin House. Photograph by W. W. Bass, 1914.

79

We kids always had quite a bit to do. My Dad tried to keep a horse up at the house at all times so we would have something to ride. I would pick grass and plants, pick these during the day, and then when I came in at night, I'd have one, maybe two sacks full of grass for the horse and we wouldn't have to turn it out.

But we didn't always have hay for all the horses, and someone had to go out and herd them all day, watch over them. When I was out ranging, I often took my horse and rode all around. I'd go up on a high hill where nobody could hear me and I'd try to sing and just shake my voice, to make sure of my voice, while I was on top of the hill with the horses all around and just sing. . . .

Range on the south rim. Date and photographer unknown.

81

My Dad didn't have any mules, only horses and burros. Tried to leave the burros, as many as he could, to make their own way down in the Canyon, to find their own water someplace. Less to take care of, have on top. He tried to keep enough tame burros in the wild herds though, to keep them there for emergency so if we needed a burro down there, we could always get one.

There was a certain number of them in the pasture on top, too. But if the burros were around the house when we were talking inside about rounding them up to go down the Canyon the next day, why, in the morning you couldn't find any of them. They had gone to hide someplace.

I believe, I really do, they understood us because the same thing happened always. So we were very careful how we talked in front of the burros, unless we wanted to spend hours hunting them the next day.

Burros on the north side of the Colorado, below Bass Rapid. Photograph by F. H. Maude, circa 1898.

My Dad got a carload of fifty burros from New Mexico, got them from Laguna, I think. They brought them on the train as far as Anita, then drove them on to Bass Camp. And John named them, named every one of them as they came over the hill one by one.

At the Bass cable ferry. Photograph by F. H. Maude, circa 1908.

85

John . . . John Waltenberg was a mystery. I don't know where he came from or how he tied up with my Dad, whether they were partners or what. He just depended on my Dad to look after him.

But John was awfully good to me, more like a mother he was. He'd help me with my clothes, turn me around to see if my clothes were buttoned and things like that. And in the evening when we'd go outside and sit on the porch, why, I always climbed on John's knee and sat in his lap.

I always felt bad about John: he never realized anything from all those years of work, except a case of *Star* chewing tobacco now and then.

John Waltenberg. Studio photograph, date unknown.

I rode the burros first as a boy—they weren't so high off the ground. Then later, as I grew up, I was riding mostly horses. I still remember their names: Molly and Speck, Baldy and Bugler, Dan and Prince, and my favorite: Roany.

All our horses were broken to harness and to the saddle, too. That way we could use them for riding, driving, or packing. Sometimes when breaking the four horse teams, why, they would be pretty wild horses still, pretty frisky. My Dad would get them all harnessed up, ready to go, with the leaders blindfolded and hobbled. He'd get on the seat and my Mother, she'd pull the blindfold off and run, get on the boot of the wagon, and they'd go for several miles, jumping and running with the hobbles on until the horses got tamed out. And then she'd jump off, take the hobbles off, and get back on the front seat.

On the Topacobya trail. Photograph by F. H. Maude, 1899.

My Dad was always trying to improve his stock. He had some copper-bottoms, standard-breds, and steel-dusts. Copper-bottoms were carriage horses. Steel-dusts were the forerunners of the quarter horse. Standard-breds were good pacers.

One year he bought a horse, a dapple-gray Percheron stallion called Levi. Paid $500 and twenty-six copper-bottoms for it. They brought him over to the White House, and we kept him there in the corral for a few months. Then John took him out to Bass Camp and let him go there at the cisterns so he'd know where to go for water. Had a bell around his neck so we would always know where he was.

Less than a year later he was dead, killed by a little scrub Indian stallion. It was in May, and I remember that evening when he didn't come in with the horses, and my Dad went out and found him dead, killed there. And I remember my Dad bringing home his bloody collar with the bell on it and he was crying. . . .

We never got any colts out of the Percheron. He was a strange horse in a strange country with too much competition.

Horses near Bass Camp. Photograph by F. H. Maude, date unknown.

91

My Dad bought his first car in 1914. He had always used Studebaker wagons, liked them real well, so when he bought his first car, it was a Studebaker.

Several times he tried to learn to drive. I got my chauffeur's license a couple years after he bought that car, and I tried to teach him one time. We were going from Grand Canyon down to the White House five miles away. My Dad was sitting behind the wheel, he was driving. We had to turn around at one place where the ground was kind of flat, so I told him to turn up there, at that tree, and stop. But he got excited and put his foot on the accelerator instead of the brake and, as the car speeded up, why, he pulled back on the steering wheel and hollered "Whoa!" and hit the tree.

Then I decided to teach my Mother to drive, but she'd get to looking around the countryside and didn't watch where she was going. So they both gave up and neither one of them learned to drive.

W. W. Bass, Ada Bass, and Bill at Bass Camp in the family's first car. Photograph by Ed Kahle, 1914.

One time my Dad and my Mother started for the Canyon with a team, from Wickenburg. A day or two later I too left, with the car, and caught up with them in Ashfork. Then I went on to the Canyon. It was in the fall and a snowstorm was coming. When I got to the Canyon, Bert Lauzon, who was married to Edith by then, said he was afraid for them. "Let's go get them," he said. We threw his saddle in the car and started back. We met them down on the Cataract, my Mother and Dad on this old wagon, cold as the dickens. We put the yoke in the car and wired the tongue to the back. Bert saddled one of the horses because he had to ride them in. I put my Mother in the car, and Dad rode on the wagon to put the brakes on. It was the fastest ride he ever had on a wagon.

On the south rim. Date and photographer unknown.

I like to think of him this way, gauntlets and all, sitting there on the rim when he had six wagons and two cars taking tourists on drives, and every time you'd see a crowd on the rim you knew Bass was there.